BURIED BENEATH US

DISCOVERING THE ANCIENT CITIES OF THE AMERICAS

ANTHONY AVENI

ILLUSTRATED BY
KATHERINE ROY

ROARING BROOK PRESS NEW YORK

To all the American teachers who venture with their students into the worlds of the past and those of other cultures —A.A.

For Mom and Dad, who encouraged me to keep digging —K.R.

Text copyright © 2013 by Anthony Aveni
Illustrations copyright © 2013 by Katherine Roy
Roaring Brook Press is a division of Holtzbrinck Publishing Holdings Limited Partnership
175 Fifth Avenue, New York, New York 10010
mackids.com

Library of Congress Cataloging-in-Publication Data
Aveni, Anthony F.
   Buried beneath us : discovering the ancient cities of the Americas / Anthony Aveni ;
illustrated by Katherine Roy.
     pages   cm
   ISBN 978-1-59643-567-4 (hardcover)—ISBN 978-1-59643-913-9 (ebook)
 1. Indians—Urban residence—Juvenile literature.   2. Indians—Dwellings—Juvenile literature. 3. Indians—
Antiquities—Juvenile literature.   4. Cities and towns—America—Juvenile literature. 5. America—
Antiquities—Juvenile literature.   I. Roy, Katherine, illustrator.   II. Title.
   E59.C55A84 2013
   970.01—dc23
                                                                                    2012046757

Roaring Brook Press books may be purchased for business or promotional use. For information on bulk
purchases please contact Macmillan Corporate and Premium Sales Department at (800) 221-7945 x5442 or by
email at specialmarkets@macmillan.com.

First edition 2013
Book design by Andrew Arnold
Printed in China by South China Printing Co. Ltd., Dongguan City, Guandong Province

10 9 8 7 6 5 4 3 2 1

CONTENTS

①

WHAT ARE CITIES?

Downtown Mexico City, the largest city in the Americas, February 21, 1978: Electrical workers are at work laying a cable on a busy street corner. Suddenly a loud clank resonates from the tip of a laborer's shovel. Kicking away the surrounding dirt, he realizes the edge of the stone he has struck is round and far too huge to dislodge. He calls over his fellow workers to help out. Further digging reveals a portion of a carved arm, then an upturned face five times bigger than life, with a tasseled headdress adorned with bells.

Archaeologists from the nearby National Institute of Anthropology and History are called in. Jumping into the pit, they quickly abandon the shovels and get to work with their trowels and whisk brooms so as not to damage the delicate carving. They employ dental picks and toothbrushes to chip away caked-on dirt.

Previous and following pages: The excavation of the Coyolxauhqui Stone, found in 1978 at the foot of the Great Temple (or Templo Mayor) stairway, part of the Aztec capital, Tenochtítlan.

The archaeologists had found evidence of an ancient city, Tenochtítlan, that grew, thrived, flourished, and was destroyed on the turf where modern Mexico City stands today.

Over four hundred years earlier, Bernal Diaz del Castillo, a soldier accompanying Hernando Cortés, wrote on seeing Tenochtítlan for the first time: "[A]ll around me there are great towers and buildings rising from the water, all built of masonry. I do not know how to describe it, seeing things that had never before been heard of or seen before nor even dreamed about."

It's difficult to reconcile Bernal Diaz's awe over a vast, teeming city with a place that has been reduced to ruins, almost undetectable under the streets of Mexico City. Yet there are other examples of ancient cities that once existed before European settlers ever reached America's shores. In the Americas, cities have grown up, flourished, and died for three thousand years. Centuries before our modern cities appeared, great cultural centers flourished in what is now the American Midwest, Mexico, and the Andes of South America.

The first American cities rose and fell long before our contemporary urban areas blossomed, but they all created lasting works that impress us to this day—tall buildings, huge monuments, exquisitely decorated architecture, beautiful paintings, and spectacular sculpture. Some ancient cities developed writing, literature, and mathematics. Like Boston, Seattle, Los Angeles, Vancouver, and Lima today, America's ancient cities were style setters, symbols of what it meant to be modern and creative. Each developed a great tradition that was maintained for a long time, a way of living that affected and transformed many of the cultures they came in contact with. Their people embraced ideas and customs that seem very different from our own, but there is much to be learned from the ruins of their courts and temples, streets and fortifications—even the everyday articles of the people, rich and poor, who once lived there.

The many people who have inhabited our planet before us left a lasting impression on the world, and we can benefit from their knowledge. If we look closely enough, we can discover where they succeeded and why they failed. That's the lesson of history.

CAHOKIA

Five hundred years before Christopher Columbus's arrival, Cahokia was the biggest city in North America. One of the many cities of the Mississippian culture, this metropolis was made up of more than three thousand structures. Monk's Mound, the highest of them all, rises up to seventy-five feet (about five stories in a modern building). And yet this lost city lay overgrown and undiscovered until the eighteenth century.

When the American explorers Meriwether Lewis and William Clark crossed the Mississippi River going west in 1804, they spotted a tiny Indian village just south of where St. Louis is located today. Clark's diary for September 23 reads: "[We] descended to the Mississippi and round to St. Louis, where we arrived at twelve o'clock; and having fired a salute, went on shore and received the heartiest and most hospitable welcome of the whole village."

When they stepped ashore, they noticed that the shoreline was strewn with lots of broken pottery and pieces of flint arrowheads, indicating that people had already inhabited those lands. Because they were preoccupied by this social occasion, they had little time to explore the land farther from the riverbank.

What they missed, hidden deep in the brush, was a massive building covering an area of fourteen acres (that's bigger than twelve soccer fields!). The French explorers Jacques Marquette and Louis Joliet, who made that same crossing more than one hundred years earlier, had missed seeing the lost pyramid, too.

The explorers failed to recognize the great pyramid on the Mississippi because even though it stands out in the landscape, the pyramid is made of earth. It doesn't have any stone facing like Egypt's pyramids and it isn't covered over with stucco and painted in bright colors like the Mexican pyramids, so it was easy to mistake it for a natural hill.

By the time President Thomas Jefferson's good friend, the explorer Henry Brackenridge, arrived in the area in 1811, he knew what he was looking for. Brackenridge had heard that there were many Indian mounds situated on the edge of the Mississippi/Missouri floodplain, or bottomlands. He knew that a spot near the intersection of two of America's great rivers would have been an excellent place to build a city. The location offered great soil for planting and a watery highway for trading goods.

As he hacked his way inward from the shore through the cedar- and willow-covered bluffs, Brackenridge noticed that the mounds got bigger and bigger and they were regularly spaced. He had a strong feeling that he was about to arrive at some very important ancient place. Suddenly, he found himself standing in front of the huge earthen pyramid. He had discovered ancient Cahokia! Awestruck, he would later write to the president: "I was astonished that this stupendous monument of antiquity should have been unnoticed by any traveler." He named it Monk's Mound after a group of French monks who had built a monastery nearby.

Let's turn the Cahokia clock back a thousand years and try to imagine what Monk's Mound looked like in AD 1000. The earthen structure supported a huge pole and thatch temple, likely the residence of an elite class of rulers. The grass roof of the temple was decorated with wood carvings of animals covered with feathers. The great pyramid had a two-hundred-acre plaza in front of it, surrounded by a stockade made out of twenty thousand twelve-foot-long logs. That alone would have taken a crew of one hundred workers twenty years working eight hours a day to build—without a day off!

TENOCHTÍTLAN AND THE AZTECS

More than a thousand miles south of Cahokia, underneath modern Mexico City, lie the ruins of another great native American city, Tenochtítlan, the ancient capital of the Aztecs. We know more about what life was like when that city flourished more than five hundred years ago than we do about any ancient American city. That's because, unlike the people of Cahokia, the Aztecs of Mexico have left us a picture record of their history in addition to magnificent ruined temples made of stone. Before the arrival of the Spaniards, the Aztecs made books, called **codices**, out of deerskin. These books told stories about the founding of their city, how they worshipped their gods, the history of their wars, and the lives of their rulers. After the conquest of Mexico by Spain in the sixteenth century, priests who came to the New World to convert the Aztec people to Catholicism interviewed Aztec officials and acquired further details about daily life. Scribes and artists continued to create codices during the colonial period.

At the time of Spanish contact, Tenochtítlan was one of the largest cities in the world—more than fifty thousand people made their homes there.

Unlike the first explorers who visited Cahokia, the first outsiders to view Tenochtítlan saw a real live "downtown pyramid" in a bustling city. There were many temples, altars made of stone for worshipping a host of Aztec deities, schools, marketplaces, and ball courts. Seeking gold, the Spanish conqueror Hernando Cortés docked his ship in Veracruz on the Gulf of Mexico in 1519. Accompanied by a few hundred men, a few dozen horses, and warriors from tribes who considered themselves enemies of the Aztecs, Cortés climbed the pass between the snowcapped twin volcanoes called **Popocatépetl** (the man) and **Ixtaccihuatl** (the woman). It was there that Cortés first cast his eyes upon the Valley of Mexico below him. He glimpsed Tenochtítlan, the great city situated on an island in Lake **Texcoco** and connected to the mainland by four causeways. Seeing the gleaming palaces with exquisite gardens and waterways, one of his soldiers wrote in his diary: "[T]here is a building of such height and beauty that it astonishes me . . . the equal in cut stone of any I have seen in Seville, and all around there are eleven or twelve more just like it all closely clustered together." For the first time, outsiders were glimpsing an American city that rivaled the great urban centers of Europe.

CUZCO

When Francisco Pizarro and his army landed on the west coast of South America in 1532 and penetrated the high Andes to reach Cuzco, they, too, were awed by what they saw in this equally large city. It had taken them several weeks to reach the city, trekking over mountains that rose to 15,000 feet. South America's west coast presents a hostile environment—steep valleys lie between high, snow-covered peaks that crowd up against the coast. Living there might seem difficult to us, but, as in other rugged environments like the deserts of Egypt, people learn to adapt to the world around them.

And the Inca did more than just survive in this harsh environment; they flourished. They built this fourteenth-century city out of stone blocks carved, without metal tools, so perfectly that you can't fit the blade of a knife between the stone slabs that make up their buildings. They mastered the control of water in a landscape that was very difficult to irrigate, and decorated their most important places of worship in gold.

The Spaniards especially marveled at Cuzco's **Coricancha** (it means "golden enclosure"), also called the Temple of the Ancestors. It was sheathed with large plates of gold to honor the color of their sun god, Inti. The invaders greedily pried hundreds of these two-foot-square, fifty-pound plates off the stonework. But Pizarro was seeking greater treasure—the king's golden throne and tubs of silver and emeralds, which he had heard about from Indian informants. The king had hidden away most of the gold when he got word that the Spanish were marching on his capital. But Pizarro captured **Atahualpa**, king of the Inca. He promised to spare the king's life if he delivered the treasure. Pizarro ordered Atahualpa to fill a huge hall in the temple with these precious items (about 500 million dollars worth of goods in today's currency). The ruthless Pizarro painted a red line seven feet from the floor all the way around the room to show how high the pile must rise in order for the king to be spared. (You can still see it today if you visit Cuzco!)

Even though Atahualpa granted Pizarro's wish, the conqueror failed to keep his promise and had Atahualpa killed. The Inca believed all power was concentrated in their ruler. So, cutting the lifeline between the people and their king would make conquest much simpler. But as in Mexico, the conquest of Peru would not have been possible without alliances made by Pizarro with Indians who were the enemies of the Inca. If his allies had only known they were trading their local enemies for a far worse alien force!

COPÁN

The ancient Maya, who lived in the Yucatán Peninsula, have fascinated us ever since early explorers rediscovered their lost cities back in the 1830s. Travel books were popular at a time in American history when the land west of the Appalachian Mountains was being opened up to exploration. Writer John Lloyd Stephens caught the imagination of the public with his vivid descriptions, accompanied by exquisitely detailed drawings by Frederick Catherwood, which proved that remarkable cities once flourished in the mosquito-infested jungles of southern Yucatán. The thick jungle seemed to them a weird place to build cities. Stephens encountered the ruins of the ornate stuccoed buildings at the city of **Palenque** and the delicate sculpture of Copán. He also visited the stately ruins of **Uxmal** and **Chichén Itzá** in the north of Yucatán, marveling at what he saw every step of the way.

Stephens was particularly awed by the carved stelae, or standing stones, arranged around the plazas of the great Maya cities. The stelae looked like gravestones and they showed bigger than life statues of beings garbed in ornate clothing and holding long staffs. Were they gods or people, he wondered? Then he noticed strange hieroglyphs on the stelae:

> What do the stelae peeking out of the jungle depict? Here they stand, silent and solemn, strange in design, excellent in sculpture, rich in ornament—their whole history so entirely unknown, their hieroglyphics unintelligible . . . [W]ho shall read them?

2

WHERE DO CITIES COME FROM AND HOW DO THEY GROW?

The original peopling of the Americas began about twenty thousand years ago in the far north of Alaska. There, a strip of land known as the Bering land bridge connected North America to Asia. Migrants from Asia tracked game across the land bridge. In several waves of migration lasting thousands of years, they crossed what is now Canada into the United States. As the hunters and their descendants trickled down to Central America, following migrating herds of reindeer, caribou, and buffalo, and supplementing their diet with wild plants, they mixed bloods, genes, DNA, languages, and customs.

Once the land bridge disappeared beneath the ocean waves, the first Americans were here to stay. And what a diverse group of cultures they would become: Aztec, Mississippian, Inca, Maya, and many more. About five

Facing page: Early settlers in the Mississippi Valley built thatch-roofed homes in the area that would become Cahokia. Following pages: the waters of the Mississippi pass near several major American cities, serving as a trade route to transport raw materials and goods.

thousand years ago, these people began to realize the advantages of staying in one place as opposed to the nomadic life of hunting and gathering. They domesticated plants, like corn, and animals, like dogs, and began to live in small villages, where they could develop specialized skills. Archaeological evidence shows that some became skilled potters, weavers, and toolmakers. A few of the more successful settlements—the ones with the best crops and the most sought-after products—would gradually grow in population and become cities. Not every settlement grew to become a bustling city—a number of factors determined whether these population centers flourished or failed.

One key to a city's success is a good location. Proximity to an abundant supply of good drinking water is important. So is fertile land capable of producing a large supply of fruits and vegetables. Settlements founded near rivers, especially those with tributaries people can navigate, are better situated to develop opportunities to trade for a wider variety of goods over greater distances. Finally, the more defensible your location is—say surrounded by water or on a hilltop—the safer you are from attack.

America's first great cities grew out of small settlements that possessed many of these advantages. Cahokia was built on a bluff overlooking the Mississippi River, just south of where its two main tributaries joined. Cuzco was built in a fertile valley at the junction of two rivers and surrounded by high mountains. And Tenochtítlan was built on an island in the middle of a huge lake.

Modern American cities are no different. Washington, D.C., was located on the site of an old fort on the banks of the Potomac River, at the farthest point upstream that ships of the eighteenth century could safely navigate. That made it easier to trade goods from the Virginia and Maryland colonies. Most of the early colonial cities, like Boston, Philadelphia, Baltimore, Charleston, Savannah, and New Orleans, developed from tiny settlements at the water's edge into deep-water ports. New York would not have become the largest city in America if it weren't for the Erie Canal, which connected to the docks of New York, by way of the Hudson River, to the bountiful fur and grain trade from America's heartland.

Chicago was conveniently founded at the southern end of Lake Michigan. St. Louis was strategically located, too, like its ancient predecessor, Cahokia, just twenty miles downriver from the place where the Mississippi and Missouri rivers joined together. Its founder, Pierre Laclède, wrote in 1764, "I have found a situation where I am going to form a settlement which might become, hereafter, one of the finest cities in America—so many advantages are embraced in its site, by its locality and central position, for forming settlements."

Actually, planning a city wasn't so high on this Frenchman's agenda. He was more interested in selecting the best place to set up a fur trading post. He chose that particular spot because the river moved swiftly there and it did not flood, thanks to the high bluffs that overlook it from both sides. If you want to see how much of the United States is accessible by water that eventually passes by St. Louis, check out any U.S. map.

Food supply also affects a city's survival. Cities can only grow to the extent that they can feed their people. None of the early American cities could have flourished without stable, long-term access to a nutritious food supply. From collecting remains, archaeologists know that corn was the staple crop of all the North and Central American cities, from Aztec Tenochtítlan to Maya **Tikal** and Copán. Without it, these civilizations could not have survived.

corn

Corn originated in the Americas. Around 7000 BC, hunter-gatherers in the mountains of southern Mexico began to cultivate different kinds of edible grasses. One of them is called **teosinte**, the ancestor of the corn plant. As they moved with the seasons to get their food supply, the hunter-gatherers gradually began to domesticate corn. They selected the seeds of the biggest and

teosinte

heartiest teosinte. They put them in the ground and left them behind. The next year when they returned, they had food to eat. You'd have a hard time recognizing what ancient corn looked like. Teosinte cobs were about the size of your little finger. But because its seeds mutated over time, corn eventually grew to much larger sizes.

Once corn was tamed, specialized stone workers invented *manos* and *metates* to grind it into flour to make bread. That's where tortillas came from. Archaeologists find evidence of these basic kitchen tools in caves occupied as early as 5000 BC. Remains of fragile pottery dated to 3400 BC prove that by this time people had begun to settle down together in small villages, the most successful and fortunate of which would grow into cities as the population became even more specialized. Since they had enough food stored, people didn't need to move with the seasons any longer. They became sedentary farmers instead of nomadic hunter-gatherers. Maybe it was corn that tamed people!

The potato was to the South American Andes what corn was to Meso-america. To become a successful farmer in the vertical environment of the Andes, you needed to master the control of water; that is, you needed to move this precious liquid over the maximum possible acreage as it flowed down from the highlands. By terracing the land and planting in different altitudes at different seasons of the year, farmers learned to grow more than twenty differ-ent kinds of potatoes. The ancestors of the Inca, who would go on to develop South America's biggest empire, were among those hardy mountain people. There certainly were other factors involved in making them great, but were it not for the two basic crops, potatoes and corn, Cuzco and Tenochtítlan could not have succeeded.

Convenient location, easy access to resources, and protection from harm are essential to the survival of every great city, but skilled leadership is also necessary to make sure that the population benefits from these advantages. The best leaders were those who surrounded themselves with well-educated advisers who knew how to manage trade relations and resources. They would also be the ones to carefully cultivate traditions that could be shared by all who lived in the city, bringing it to life and giving the people a common identity.

The Aztec empire began when migrants known as Mexica from the north entered the fertile lands surrounding Lake Texcoco in the basin of Mexico early in the fourteenth century. Driven from one settlement area after another, they finally managed to secure an abandoned island in the middle of the lake that nobody else wanted. The island lacked good drinking water and there were few trees and rocks that they could use to build houses and temples. But the migrants were determined to make this place their home. They brought material to their island for landfill; they cut down and transported trees and stones from the mainland. They built canals and created floating gardens in the lake. They connected their island to the mainland via narrow, well-fortified causeways. The Mexica even carted carved stone and jade tens and even hundreds of miles from the abandoned sites of two ancient cities, Teotihuácan and Tula. These precious goods would give their city prestige by establishing connections with empires of a previous age. By the beginning of the fifteenth century, the Mexica had turned their island into a paradise.

"We are the offspring of the ancient city of Aztlan," one of their kings told the chief of a tribe they had recently conquered. Because Aztlan was their name for Tula, they renamed themselves the Aztecs. Only a century after its founding, the ambitious Aztecs of Tenochtítlan would subjugate all the towns surrounding Lake Texcoco.

The Aztecs told stories of their conquests in the picture books we call codices. They say that a long line of Aztec emperors reached back to the early fourteenth century, when Tenochtítlan was founded. Many carved-stone monuments in the ruins of Tenochtítlan commemorate their achievements; for example, those of King **Moctezuma** I (1440–1467), who set the Aztecs on a course of expansion by conquering the cities around the Valley of Mexico, and Kings **Axayacatl** (1469–1481) and **Ahuítzotl** (1486–1501), who expanded the empire.

Facing page: The Mexica built the city of Tenochtítlan on a swampy island in the middle of Lake Texcoco.

The Aztecs recorded their history through picture stories called codices.

19

Under Ahuitzotl, by the end of the fifteenth century the Aztecs would create a true empire, holding power over towns as far south as the Pacific coast of Guatemala and demanding tributes of gold, jade, jaguar skins, precious feathers, and cacao from them. One of the codices, the Mendoza, depicts on page after page the hordes of precious items exacted from conquered peoples by the lustful Ahuitzotl.

One of the most impressive items found buried inside the Great Temple of Tenochtítlan is a clay statue of an eagle warrior. Bigger than a human, it had to be put together in three parts. Its size alone testifies to the importance of war in the Aztec state. But many of these wars were nothing like our own. For example, the codices tell us that the Aztecs staged Flower Wars, contests arranged formally by agreement with other communities for the purpose of capturing prisoners for sacrifice. The king would challenge the enemy to send their best warriors to combat at a designated field of battle. They also had Coronation Wars to test a new emperor's leadership on the battlefield.

Cities grow in prestige by acquiring valuable resources, such as higher quality obsidian for toolmaking or the most precious jade for ornamentation. If these resources lie beyond a city's boundary, getting hold of them may make it necessary to pass through neighboring territory, so good relations with your neighbors are important. Trade agreements and alliances through intermarriage can help, but sometimes conflict can erupt into full-scale war and the takeover of one community by another. We know that this is what happened to the Maya.

A century ago, most researchers thought of the Maya as a peaceful people devoted to philosophy, art, and science. They believed the stelae found at Maya sites portrayed Maya gods, and that the numbers and glyphs carved on them dealt only with time and astronomy. Today we know that's not true. In 1960, epigrapher Tatiana **Proskouriakoff** began to suspect that Maya hieroglyphs didn't have so much to do with gods. Looking closely at the dates on Maya stelae, she noticed that when she subtracted the latest date from the earliest one carved on each of the stelae at the ruins of **Piedras Negras**, she ended up with a period of time approximately equal to the length of a human lifetime. She also noticed that the first date on a monument almost always was followed by an "upturned frog" glyph and the last by a "Q" glyph. A "toothache glyph" usually appeared somewhere in between. (Epigraphers name glyphs after what they look like; for example, a froggy face pointing upward or a face with a bandage tied around the jaw and head and knotted at the top). She made a hypothesis: the upturned frog means someone was born on the first date and the Q glyph means that person died on the last date. These portraits in stone were the stories of real people. They were the rulers, not the gods.

upturned frog
glyph = birth

toothache glyph =
accession to office

Q glyph = death

What about the dates in between? Proskouriakoff believed they referred to important events; for example, the toothache glyph denotes accession to office. Other glyphs stand for marriage, the capture of a rival chief, and so on; they are important events in the life of the ruler, whose figure is carved on the stela. Based on her hypothesis, Proskouriakoff was able to work out the three-hundred-year chronology of the dynasty that ruled Piedras Negras. Some kings and queens turn out to be just as good or bad as famous rulers we've heard of in our own history: Alexander the Great, Julius Caesar, Napoleon, Hitler. Archaeologists have dug up the tombs of many Maya kings. We now know the rulers' names as well as those of their descendants. We even know about the wars they fought.

About the same time, another epigrapher, Heinrich Berlin, noticed that inscriptions at many sites ended with a special hieroglyph that seemed to belong to that particular site. He proved that these "emblem glyphs" actually stand for the names of the cities. Emblem glyphs are like the logos—lions, dolphins, and maple leaves—that appear on team sports equipment. Sometimes the name of one city is found on a stela at another site. This could mean that the two cities traded, warred, or made marriage alliances with one another.

Copán = leaf-nosed bat   Tikal = package with ribbon   Palenque = cracked piece of stone   Calakmul = snake's head

The Maya of Yucatán never created an extended empire, but smaller Maya city-states did develop their own dynasties. The stelae tell us a lot about Maya politics. So do the elaborate stucco carvings on the huge spaces above the doorways of their temples. They also give us a sense of how Maya rulers tried to bolster the people's confidence in their right to rule. Our constitution guarantees our president that right. The Maya rulers claimed that right through their bloodline. These monumental works proclaimed the connection between the dynasty of the ruler and the ancestor gods who created the world.

The legacy of ancient writing systems gives us deep insights into history. Today, epigraphers have deciphered more than half the hieroglyphs on the Maya monuments. For the first time, they are able to tell us something about the history and politics of the Maya. For example, we know that Tikal, positioned along several trade routes at the center of Yucatán, was the largest

Maya city from AD 400–600. It had taken over the territory of the central **Petén** rain forest by defeating rival **Uaxactún** in a fierce war in the fourth century. Later, Tikal conquered many nearby cities. Meanwhile, **Calakmul** was building its own rival city to the north. In AD 657, Calakmul attacked Tikal. Though he was unable to defeat the Tikal king, the Calakmul ruler did embarrass him by taking over many of the towns he had controlled between the two cities. Then in AD 695, Tikal struck back and defeated Calakmul, capturing its ruler. At the eastern end of the Maya world, a ruler named **Yax Pasah** (New Sun at Horizon) proclaimed himself the proud descendant of ancient Maya rulers, whose stelae are distributed all over the ruins of Copán. Yax Pasah traced his lineage back four hundred years to Copán's first ruler, **Yax K'uk' Mo'** (Resplendent **Quetzal** Macaw), who came from far away Teotihuácan. The century that lay ahead would be a difficult one, with more warfare and even bigger problems that would help trigger the great Maya collapse and the eventual end of the Maya cities.

The four emblem glyphs discovered most often on Maya stelae are Copán (which looks like the head of a leaf-nosed bat), Tikal (a package tied with a ribbon), Palenque (a cracked piece of stone), and Calakmul (a snake's head). These also happen to be among the largest Maya cities. Archaeologists call these big cities super-states because they dominated the smaller towns in a large area around them. Like Ahuitzotl, skillful Maya rulers knew that conquering and subjugating neighboring populations guards a city against future attack. Stelae at the smaller cities (called vassal sites in carved inscriptions found at these locations) tell about

An offering is made to a Maya king.

the gift tributes these tiny communities were required to pay to their larger, more powerful neighbors. These often consisted of the precious goods sought by the rulers in the first place. Many such offerings have been dug out of royal tombs, along with elaborately decorated painted vases showing what the inside of a king's palace looked like. Painted vessels depict scenes with servants offering a king exotic food as he sits on his throne. Visitors or courtiers are also shown paying him tribute. These scenes tell us that rulers even at tiny cities were held in very high regard and probably thought of by the residents as divine.

The Inca also entered into territorial disputes. Not surprisingly, their wars were most often fought over the control of waterways in the difficult mountain environment where they ruled. Because it was strategically situated at the junction of two major rivers, Cuzco often got involved in resolving disputes among neighboring towns; but rulers took advantage of the situation where they could—like demanding tributes from each of the warring tribes. Once they had acquired a large number of subjects, the Inca organized the people into eighty provinces. Unlike the Aztec empire, in which acquiring material things was primary, each province was given a feeling of independence by being allowed to have its own local ruler. To help keep the peace, the Inca cleverly relocated loyal subjects in hostile territories so that they could calm the enemy. They moved the most rebellious people to territories far away in the empire where they would cause less trouble. The Inca even established a special secret language, called **Runa Simi**, for conducting all their government business.

The Inca were amazing organizers and this had much to do with the success of their city. In the early fifteenth century, the Inca extended family, led by the great king Pachacuti Inca, built a dynasty that had come to dominate the other highland tribes in their vicinity. Within two generations, Pachacuti had established the highest empire in the world (more than two miles high!). They ruled over twelve million people in the southern half of their empire from their great capital city of Cuzco, which they called **Tahuantinsuyu**, "city of the four directions." They thought of it as the "navel of the world" and the ruler lay at its center. Your navel is your birthline—the place where the umbilical cord that gave you life before birth once connected you to your mother. So for the Inca, Tahuantinsuyu was the world's lifeline.

Despite the forbidding landscape, the Inca developed the largest empire in the Americas, linking it by 25,000 miles of roads that ran from Ecuador to Argentina. It might have lasted hundreds of years if it hadn't been so violently interrupted by the invaders from Europe.

Inca foot messengers could relay news at a speed of 150 miles a day, using the empire's network of roads and grass bridges.

In Cuzco, the idea of a *balanced* universe was the key to governing people successfully. The founder of the dynasty, Pachacuti Inca, took advantage of the organizing principle of *paired opposites* (**moieties**) to keep the Inca empire together.

He divided the capital city into two moieties, two halves that complemented each other. He called them Hanan Cuzco, or upper Cuzco, because it lay north of the river junction toward the source of water, and Hurin Cuzco, or lower Cuzco, which lay in the downhill direction, south of the junction.

If you think about it, most things come in pairs: day and night, left and right, male and female. There are many other examples. The Inca believed opposites, like man and woman, wet and dry, hot and cold, didn't conflict with, but rather strengthened one another. There was a *reciprocal* relationship or a balance between them. Opposites *complemented* each other. They built a city and an empire on that premise. For example, to have a successful economy the Inca rulers realized that they needed to bring together the products of the high and the low places that made up their environment. From the mountain highlands came many varieties of potatoes and tubers that they farmed, along

with **llamas** and **alpacas** that grazed on the **puna** (the high plateaus). From the lowlands on the coast came the cotton, cactus, fruit, and squash that they grew, and the fish that they caught in the sea. Cuzco developed a two-part moiety system of commerce. This allowed the city to draw from these diverse ecological environments, which ensured that citizens would have access to a wide range of resources. It also offered some insurance against crop failures or natural disasters, like floods and earthquakes, which were common in the Andes.

In addition to dividing their capital into moieties, the Inca further organized Cuzco by splitting it up like a pie into forty-one zones that outlined the path of the water that flowed into and out of the capital. These zones were defined by lines, called *ceques*, which went out like spokes on a wheel from the Coricancha. Ceques were invisible lines, but each could be traced out by a series of *huacas*, or sacred places (there were 328 in all). At these places, the people made their offerings to the gods. If you've ever made a

Ceque lines radiated out from the Coricancha, the golden temple at the center of ancient Cuzco, to the city's 328 sacred sites.

connect-the-dots drawing, you'll get the idea. The Inca thought of these huacas as openings in the body of **Pachamama** (Mother Earth), who nurtured all people. You could think of the ceques as the veins through which Pachamama's blood (water really) flows. So Cuzco really was a living city!

To establish a sense of community, the rulers of Cahokia celebrated elaborate festivals. Cahokia had a giant clock to mark the festival days. Archaeologists call it Woodhenge, a circle four hundred feet in diameter consisting of forty-eight posts. The archaeologists who named it believe Cahokia priests used Woodhenge as a giant sun calendar. There's a posthole placed off center. If you stand at that point on certain key dates in the Cahokian calendar, the sun appears over the proper post for that holiday.

Cahokia's biggest holiday of the year happened in mid-July. Called the Busk Festival, after a Creek Indian word meaning a fast that takes place before

the new crop, this special day was dedicated to the green corn. The ceremony occurred a month after the June solstice, the first day of summer, when the sun stands highest in the sky at noon.

On this occasion, fifteen thousand people would crowd into the plaza. They came from near and far to celebrate the green corn ritual. Other outsiders came to Cahokia for the ceremony, too. There were traders carrying baskets of chert from distant quarries to exchange for local products, like salt and bear teeth, and merchants who had come to the city market earlier to argue and barter to get the best deals for their pearls and shells, arrowheads, fancy digging sticks, pots and copper jewelry, and foods like pumpkins, herbs, and fish.

At noon, the chief of the people who lived in the city and its tributaries would emerge from his temple dressed in a feather robe and headdress. From his neck hung a heavy shell necklace with a shell pendant carved with the effigy of Eagle Man—his spirit-animal guide. The chief would make an offering to the gods and announce that the corn was ripe. Let the harvest begin!

Then followed a long procession of representatives from smaller nearby Indian towns to pay tribute to the chief. They offered him gifts of copper, shell, polished chunks of obsidian, lead, and mica. The celebration would go on late into the night as pine torches around the stockade lit the plaza. Everyone feasted on the first corn. Corn was as important to the Mississippians as it was to the Maya.

Strong centralized government was key to all of these cities' growth and success. Clever leaders established stable relations with the world outside the city while at the same time giving those who lived in the city a sense of belonging. But the daily life of the city was carried out in the activities of the thousands of subjects those leaders ruled. What was it like to be one of those citizens, living day to day in the ancient city?

Facing page: Woodhenge served as a calendar for Cahokia and marked important dates such as festivals and harvests. Following pages: Every July the inhabitants of Cahokia and the surrounding countryside celebrated the Busk Festival with dancing and feasts of corn.

3

DAILY LIFE IN THE CITY

Although all cities that flourish depend on good government and strong rulers, it is ultimately the people who live in cities that make them function—skilled farmers, artisans, and builders, as well as traders, who can establish extensive trade routes. To learn the skills that are required for their occupations, all productive citizens need a good education. They need to eat well and engage in vigorous physical activity to stay healthy. To build a productive community, sound government needs to provide for the welfare of its citizens.

Unfortunately, we don't know enough about the ordinary people who served as the backbone of America's first great cities. While most kings and queens lived in palaces made of stone, a building material that holds up well over time and leaves ample remains for archaeologists to dig up, ordinary citizens built

Facing page: Daily life for the Maya in the village of Joya de Cerén, in modern day Honduras.

their houses out of wood, straw, and other perishable materials. But sometimes archaeologists get lucky. Payson Sheets was one of them. One day in 1978 a bulldozer accidentally uncovered the remains of a Maya house in the small community of **Cerén**, El Salvador, where he had been working. It had been buried by ash from a volcanic eruption in the sixth century. The house was made out of wood and thatch and looked just like most houses Maya people live in today. Because the ash that covered the wood had preserved it, Sheets and his team were able to reconstruct the house, its kitchen and storerooms, even the burial places of relatives and the garden just outside. His workers found grinding stones, pottery vessels full of food, and plates with uneaten meals still on them. The house's occupants must have been surprised by the eruption.

Maya archaeologists also have learned something about common people by making settlement surveys. For example, on the outskirts of a city, they might stake out strips of land up to five miles long and just a few yards wide. By collecting broken pieces of ceramics, seeds, animal bones, and so on, along those narrow strips, they can get an idea of the population distribution. From these surveys, we know that the ancient Maya diet consisted of maize, beans, squash, and chili, and that less wealthy people lived on the outer edges of cities. Archaeologists also have learned that close to 90 percent of the people who lived in and around the great Maya cities were members of farming families. They were the ones who grew the corn, caught the fish, and traded the salt and other items that supported the Maya economy.

Decorative bowls and arrowheads from the Cahokia settlement.

Archaeological excavations have given us a glimpse of everyday life in Cahokia as well. We know Cahokians made two kinds of pottery: undecorated, or utilitarian, for the household; and decorated, or ceremonial, usually for burials or gifts to honor an important person or ancestor. The Mississippian people had lots of technological artifacts, too: hoes made out of wood and stone, shells and the shoulder bones of large animals for scraping and digging, shell cups and bowls, copper and bone fishhooks, and drills, knives, and grinding stones to process corn, which they acquired from their neighbors to the south.

Facing page: Archaeologists at Joya de Cerén uncovered the remains of corn rows and kitchens with ceramic containers still full of food.

For the Aztecs, what the archaeological record can't tell us about how ordinary people lived is more than made up for by the legacy of codices, one of the most important of which is the Mendoza Codex. It was commissioned by the first Spanish governor of Mexico, Antonio de Mendoza, in 1541. He wanted to get a firsthand account of the lives of the Aztec people while they were still alive. The first part of the Mendoza tells the history of Aztec conquests; the second part, you'll recall, shows the tributes paid to the Aztec emperors by the tribes. But the most interesting part comes last. It illustrates vivid scenes in the daily lives of typical Aztec people.

Aztec growing-up rituals began at the age of four. Up to that time, boys and girls wore the same clothes. Then boys were given their first cape and instructed always to keep it neatly tied over one shoulder. In the month of **Izcalli** ("Growth Month"), a boy's ears would be pierced. He would make his first sacrifice by having blood drawn from his earlobe with a flint knife. Then the priests would lift him up by gripping his forehead. They would pull on his arms, his ears, and his nose to encourage him to grow. In **Nahuatl**, the language spoken by the Aztec, "to educate" means "to grow."

Good Aztec parents trained their children never to be idle. Aztec kids would accompany their mother and father to the *tianquiztli* (marketplace) once a week to sell their goods. There they learned about local foods, like algae, spirulina (waterfly) eggs, and ducks from the lake, and the special things that come from far away: birds from **Atzcapotzalco**, feathers from **Cholula**, painted gourds from Texcoco. Boys would carry loads of wood to be used for fuel at home. To help keep the market tidy, they would pick up the corn and beans and other goods that the merchants had spilled. Girls learned to spin and how to make tortillas. Their parents

An Aztec girl hand-spins thread for weaving.

showed the children how to greet people in the marketplace; how to walk with straight posture and keep their feet from kicking up too high; and how to speak softly, never hurriedly. "People do not like squeakers or growlers," goes an Aztec saying.

When children misbehaved, parents brought out the thorns. The codices tell us that kids who tried to run away from school would be punished by having their hands and feet bound and maguey cactus spines stuck in their shoulders and buttocks overnight for punishment. If you didn't do your homework, you might be forced to inhale chili smoke.

The most important day in the life of an Aztec boy was his fifteenth birthday. That's when he took the single biggest step toward growing up—entering the *cuicacalli,* the preparatory school known as the "House of Song." The cuicacalli stands next to the Great Temple in the center of the island city of Tenochtítlan.

Imagine the boy entering a large patio surrounded by the dorm rooms where he will live for the next two years. Priests dressed in their elegant robes walk the halls. They are the wise men who will become his teachers. They will teach him song, poetry, and dance. Those verses, those steps, will guide him in understanding the history of his great city and his religious responsibilities.

How well a boy did in the cuicacalli reflected on all members of his family. If he achieved high honors—the Aztec called it *yollopíltic,* which means "ennobled heart"—he would add magical fire to the power and reputation of the family. If he proved to be an outstanding student, he would graduate to the *calmecac,* or the "file of houses." In the calmecac, the boy would train to become a warrior or a priest, the most respected professions in the land. He would learn the laws and the mathematics of the sacred calendar written in the codices. He would learn to play the *teponaztli,* the drum that sings out to the gods at night, and his teachers would show him how to incense a shrine and make a pilgrimage to the sacred mountains that surrounded his city.

In addition to learning about the practical tasks that their city needed to fulfill in order to function, there was also a cultural and moral component to what was taught in schools. Aztec discipline may seem pretty strict to us, but the Aztecs believed it was necessary, that it was their special task—they called it their "burden"—to keep the world in balance. To do that, you needed strict self-discipline. Everyone was required to adhere to the same social principles in order to keep the city going. Teaching children to participate in rites dedicated to the gods, the ancestors who gave Tenochtítlan the right to rule in the first place, was a major part of the moral side of the Aztec educational system.

Future warriors learned to experience pain by bleeding themselves. They also needed to pass many tests. The "fasting test" required them to eat nothing for five or ten days at a time to develop willpower; the "staying awake at night test" taught them never to sleep too much or to be lazy. They learned to acquire strength by carrying heavier and heavier loads of wood in the "physical endurance test."

Many of the more mundane subjects studied in schools in ancient American cities were not so different from what you study today—art, social studies, and the natural world. Math skills were especially important. The better prepared students were, the better they would function in specialized jobs like keeping records of goods traded and stored and making complex calculations involving timekeeping and the calendar. In Tenochtítlan, records and calculations were kept on documents made out of tanned animal skin, but in the Andean world, knotted strings were employed.

An Aztec boy plays a *teponaztli.*

One Spanish chronicler tells us that all the information about Cuzco's ceque system of organization was preserved in a strange form of writing called a **quipu**. He called them "knots that talk," and described them as "a complicated device composed of colored knots." These long sets of connected cords woven out of cotton look like old string mops. Inca authorities, called **quipucamayoc**, or quipu experts, used them for accounting and tax collecting. They kept an inventory by draping the quipus on wooden racks, the way we stack books in a library. Then they could look up accounts of items owned, taxes paid, days worked, etc. You can think of a quipu as a journal or diary. But one chronicler tells us some quipus were used to write their histories and to keep their "religious secrets." For this reason, some scholars believe that there is a code of the quipu that goes beyond numbers. Maybe it's real writing! We don't know because the code of the quipu has yet to be cracked.

Deciphering a quipu is like reading a combination of visible writing, like the words on this page, and Braille, where you need to feel the knots with your fingers to get the message. The knots are arranged in groups on long cords called pendants, because they hang from a main cord. Each group is composed of one to ten knots that are read from top to bottom. Quipus are often found bundled inside mummies found in graves. Each probably holds a record of the wealth of the individual buried there—how many llamas he owned, children he fathered, taxes

Inca farmers made knots on the strings of their quipus to keep track of harvests.

he paid, etc. But other features of quipus are still a mystery. Sophisticated quipus have many pendant cords, a huge variety of knots, lots of different colors, and even different windings of thread. Also, many sub-cords hang from the pendants.

Math learned in Maya schools was different from ours, too. Clues about just how different come from Maya codices, only a few of which survived destruction by the Spaniards. Painted on processed tree bark, they were mostly books about divination or communicating with the ancestor gods. The Maya codices gave precise time schedules for making offerings. Some were complicatedalmanacs that warned of eclipses and followed the courses of the celestial gods, such as the planets Venus and Mars. Because of their regular recurrence, the numbers are the easiest inscriptions in the codices to decipher. Dots represent ones; bars are fives; and a closed fist or shell symbol stands for zero. Numbers were written from top to bottom in a system called base 20 (our number system is based on 10s), probably because before they developed writing, the Maya were used to counting on their fingers and toes. The position at the bottom is the unit position; above it is the 20 position, then 20 x 20, or 400, with the 8,000 position on top; however, when the Maya counted *days*, instead of *things*, the 400s became 360 and the 8,000s became 20 x 360s, or 7,200s, etc. Because the Maya paid close attention to their cycles of days and numbers, this complex system was taught in the most elite schools in order to train scribes.

Sports were also important in all the ancient American cities, where people young and old participated. But they didn't play soccer, football, hockey, or baseball. Their games had odd names like *chunkey* and *pok-ta-pok*. In Cahokia, kids played the game of chunkey on special feast days. A chunkey stone is a highly polished disk about the size of a grownup's hand. Mississippians used them in a game like bowling. You took turns rolling chunkey stones down a long dirt court. Opponents threw long spears at the place where they thought the stone would stop. Whoever came closest got a point. This game must have been pretty important because archaeologists have found highly polished chunkey stones in Indian graves. You can still see the nick marks on the sides of some of the stones where spears struck them.

Think of a sport that combines basketball and soccer and you'll get an idea of what the Mesoamerican ball game of pok-ta-pok was like. Players were allowed to strike a six-pound, solid rubber ball only with their knees, hips, and shoulders. Scoring a goal was difficult because you needed to put the ball through a stone ring that could be as high as twenty-eight feet above the court. (For comparison, on modern basketball courts the hoop is ten feet above the floor.) Uniforms included heavy padding. If you slid along the court to deliver a hip shot without it, you'd get a good scraping (some people believe

Facing page: A scribe writes numbers and hieroglyphs in a codex. Top: Boys playing the game of chunkey in the city of Cahokia.

players actually wore huge U-shaped stone yokes around their waists). But even if you needed to be in great shape to play, the Mesoamerican ball game was as much about religion as it was about sports. The game was actually part of a ritual to celebrate the cycles of celestial bodies that keep time and the universe in motion. The capital-I-shaped pok-ta-pok court represented the sky, and the back and forth motion of the ball reminded spectators of the cycles of the sun, which marked the days and the seasons. The sculptures found along the wall of the ball court at the Maya ruins of Chichén Itzá give us clues about what might have happened when the game was over. It may be that somebody was sacrificed to the ancestor gods during the postgame show. Could it be the losers? We don't really know.

There is one sport we engage in today that was invented in ancient North America. We know it was played by the Indians of Virginia when the Jamestown colony was founded in 1607, and it was probably played in ancient Cahokia as well. You can probably identify it from this description in an early letter from a colonist:

> Another game is with a crooked stick, and ball made of leather stufft with hair; he wins that drives it from the other between two trees appointed for the goal.

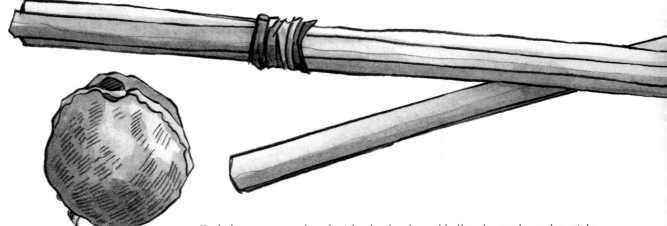

Early lacrosse was played with a leather-bound ball and netted wooden sticks.

They called it *pa-ki-ta*. Once they added a net to the end of the stick, it became lacrosse. The colonists tell of rival villages engaging one another on a neutral, level playing field between the towns. A pair of trees served as goalposts. The goals could be as much as a mile apart if there wasn't much vegetation in between. The game could last all day—there were no time-outs, and there were many injuries. According to one witness:

> Legs and arms are broken, and it has even happened that a player has been killed. It is quite common to see someone crippled for the rest of his life who would not have had the misfortune but for his own obstinancy.

Serious, crippling injury was more likely to occur when a player trapped the ball on the ground between his feet.

If you're put off by the violence in some of these games, remember that they served a purpose in each culture that played them. In ancient America, games were a way to settle arguments; they were diplomatic tools. Like the Aztec Flower Wars, they prevented wasting valuable time conducting constant warfare. By agreement, a contest allowed rival social groups to resolve territorial disputes. Ritualized battles reinforced political fellowship. This is why they arranged the events at convenient times in the carefully regulated seasonal calendar. Games might be played on seasonal agricultural festivals or on the occasion of a celestial happening, such as an eclipse.

Pok-ta-pok and lacrosse were also mechanisms for socialization. They promoted stability in the community by appealing to tradition. Every group had its own mythology about the first ball game that was played by the gods of creation. Players volleying the ball back and forth over the land believed they were reenacting the movement of the sun and the moon across the sky back in the days when the gods played the game. So, sports taught players about more than team spirit and the need to work together.

There is still much that we don't know about ordinary people in America's ancient cities. For example, what did the Maya who lived in houses in Cerén really think about their rulers? Did they regard themselves as members of the same extended family, or were they socially separate? Did people question why they should be loyal to their ruler? Were there large communal lands or did each small family unit hold on to its own small property? Was there a chance of moving up the social hierarchy? Did the state reward peasants who were skilled in art, business, or trade? Once these questions about life in the ancient cities are answered, we will have even more to reflect on about our own lives.

We do know that one of the most important aspects of daily life in America's first great cities was the practice of religion. Elaborate religious rituals served as the glue that kept people together and gave them a sense of belonging in the place where they lived.

Following pages: Maya athletes believed that pok-ta-pok was a reenactment of celestial games played by the gods.

4

HOW RELIGION KEEPS CITIES TOGETHER

Tenochtítlan, Cuzco, Cahokia, and all the Maya cities grew to great urban centers when clever and ambitious rulers like Ahuitzotl, Pachacuti Inca, Yax K'uk' Mo', and the unnamed rulers of Cahokia took advantage of fertile landscapes, mastered irrigation, and educated their citizens so that they could create productive specialized crafts. They also developed trade networks and amassed great wealth, often by taxing the weaker population centers around them. But there is one binding force no thriving ancient city could do without—religion.

The foundations of religious worship probably go back to Paleolithic times. Humans have always depended on the proliferation of other species in order to survive. Their will to live transformed the animals they hunted and the plants they gathered into objects of veneration. How did it happen?

Facing page: Aztec deer dancers used costumes and props to act out favorable hunts and seek approval from the gods.

Early tribes realized that fertility in the landscape waxed and waned; abundance turned to scarcity as heat changed to cold and rain to drought. To chart the cycle of life, early settlers created simple calendars. They kept time by the phases of the moon and the positions of sunrise and sunset over familiar landmarks. When they anticipated the appearance of a particular plant or animal, with the spring growth or a migrating herd, they celebrated with ceremonies that consisted of dramas in which they acted out the outcome they desired. They danced a deer dance at the beginning of hunting season or sang a rainmaking song at the end of the dry season. As they transformed the objects of nature around them into deities, worshippers would periodically gather to pay the debt owed the deer or rain god through sacrifice; in other words, they would give up something in return for what was given them. As settled life grew, religion would become the backbone that kept people together. Because everyone participated in the rituals, religion shaped the common identity of those who lived in the city.

But the evidence tells us that religious practices also shaped the structure of cities. It affected the construction of buildings, even down to the orientation of streets and pyramids.

Unlike those of us who follow Judaism, Christianity, and Islam, the religions associated with America's first great cities sacrificed to many gods. They were *polytheistic*, rather than *monotheistic*. (Think of the Greek deities like Athena, the goddess of wisdom, and Dionysus /Bacchus, the god of wine, and you get the idea.) It makes sense because the ancients lived very close to the diverse forces of nature: wind and water, lightning and thunder. They closely observed the different traits of plants and animals—the swiftness of the deer, the grace of the eagle, the strength of the jaguar—and believed that each force had its own creative spirit. Consider the Aztec deities, for example. Piltzintecuhtli created deer power, Xolotl created frog power, and there were two different gods associated with scorpions, one in charge of black and the other of yellow scorpion power.

Aztec gods were as colorful and varied as they were numerous. Huitzilopochtli was the most important Aztec deity. He was their *tutelary* god, a special patron whose main job it was to look after the people of Tenochtítlan. The Aztecs believed he was a sun god and one of their ancestors. But clever rulers also established him as the Aztec god of war when they began to build their empire, justifying war and conquest by making it a part of sun worship. Tlaloc, the god of rain and fertility, was worshipped all over ancient Mexico. He appeared in many forms. For example, in one of the codices he is shown bringing different kinds of rain to the crops: soft misty rain, stinging flinty rain, cold icy rain. **Tezcatlipoca** was called the "Smoking Mirror Lord." According to Aztec legend, he was once a wizard who could look into a polished obsidian mirror strapped to his foot and see into the future. Tezcatlipoca knew what you were thinking because he could also use his mirror to peer into your mind, heart, and soul.

Many of the ancient American religions were bound by cults that specialized in worshipping specific deities. While everyone in Tenochtítlan worshipped Huitzilopochtli above all other deities, other gods had their own cults. One chronicler tells us there were ninety-six cultic temples dedicated to a host of deities spread about Tenochtítlan. While we might think of the word *cult* as a negative term, for the Aztecs a cult was just a group of people from a particular walk of life, like merchants or farmers or weavers, who paid special tribute to the deity in charge of something that they were deeply concerned about. Often people belonged to more than one cult. In polytheistic systems, cults provide social cohesiveness. They

An Aztec artist makes a small carving of Huitzilopochtli, the patron god of Tenochtítlan.

allow small communities to develop a special sense of identity and belonging.

Attached to the religious rituals was a common set of beliefs grounded in myths or stories of creation that told where a city's ancestors came from and why they were special. These stories and the symbols attached to them formed the basis of a city's beliefs and traditions. Creation stories helped give citizens a shared identity. Some elements of these stories were true, and others were exaggerated just to make a good story. Creation stories are as important to modern American culture as they were to the first Americans. The tradition of twenty-first-century America is founded in the idea of democracy—we tell stories of our founding fathers, men who rebelled against an unjust king and wrote the Declaration of Independence and later the U.S. Constitution, to guarantee our freedom. A perfect example of a creation story that has been exaggerated to teach lessons about our founding principles is the story of George Washington chopping down the cherry tree. Many cultures identify their origins with sacred places that have existed since ancient times—cities like Mecca or Jerusalem. These ancient places help establish a city's tradition by giving depth to its history and a secure sense that their beliefs have endured for many ages. These stories are designed to make people feel special and, above all, to unite them.

The Aztec story of creation became a part of the tradition of Tenochtítlan because it explained why warfare and sacrifice were necessary. The purpose of the story was to justify acquiring sacrificial victims to offer in payment to the sun god so that the people could help to keep the world in balance. The Aztec's sacred place, where they say the story occurred, was an ancient city located twenty-five miles northeast of Tenochtítlan that had been abandoned long before the Aztecs arrived in the Valley of Mexico. Its giant pyramids were arranged along a ceremonial way they called the Avenue of the Dead. They named the ruined city Teotihuácan. It means "City of the Gods" or the "Place Where One Becomes Deified" in Nahuatl, the Aztec language. Using

Facing page: The Aztecs identified the Pyramid of the Sun in Teotihuácan as a place to worship their ancestors.

radiocarbon dating, archaeologists discovered that a thousand years before the Aztecs built their Great Temple of Tenochtítlan, the people of Teotihuácan had constructed their gigantic Pyramid of the Sun. It measures 740 feet, or more than two soccer fields across at its base, and is about 240 feet high. (That's nearly half the height of the Washington Monument.) The Aztecs believed that the ancient ones who lived there were their gods. One of them told the Spanish conquerors: "It is said that when all was in darkness, when yet no sun had shone and no dawn had broken—it is said—the gods gathered themselves there at Teotihuácan. There they created the fifth sun."

Here's the story: All the gods had gathered at Teotihuácan after the world had been plunged into darkness at the end of the previous creation. But before they could create humans, one of them needed to sacrifice himself by walking into the cosmic fire. Only the brave one who dared do so would become the new sun. Handsome gods, warrior gods, gods dressed in glittering jade—all of them contemplated making the sacrifice. One or two even walked to the edge of the world just beyond the pyramids and peered down at the blazing inferno that would become the rising sun. But all of them were frightened and drew back.

Then Nanauatzin, the "pimply one," stepped forward. He was a scrawny god the others often made fun of. Surprisingly and without hesitation, he dove headfirst into the raging flames and sacrificed himself. Then he rose in the east to light the world for the newly created people who could then build their own city—a place to worship their gods.

The Aztecs sacrificed to repay the gods for what they had done. Every fifty-two years, the Aztecs held the New Fire Ceremony. They put out all their fires and plunged the city into total darkness. They would throw out their mats and clean and purify their houses and patios. Priests dressed in their outfits to impersonate the gods. They climbed to the top of Citlaltepec, the Hill of the Star, to watch for the sign from the heavens that the gods would grant the world a new cycle of time when the Pleiades star group passed overhead. Aztec families would follow the parade up the mountain to witness the most important part of the ritual— kindling a fire in the breast of a sacrificial victim who had been captured in battle.

First, the priest would read an account of the first creation from his sacred book; then just as the Pleiades passed overhead they would place the victim on his back, over a curved stone in the temple doorway. One priest held an obsidian knife. He slashed open the victim's chest. He removed the heart and held it up to the gods as debt payment. Then he cast the heart into the fire. He drew out some of the fire with a pine stick and kindled it in the breast of the victim. Then he lit other pine torches from that fire and passed them to all the citizens. Finally, the New Fire was carried back down to the city by all the families and into each of their homes to light the hearth.

For the Aztecs, there was a relationship between sacrifice and creation. They believed the world needed to be renewed over and over again, and only *people* had the power to make this happen. The Aztec "New Year" ceremony linked the people directly to the process of renewal— not just of the world, but of life itself. They called themselves the children of the sun because their burden was to keep the sun on its course and their delicate world in balance.

Aztec priests lighting pine torches during the New Fire Ceremony on the Hill of the Star.

Because corn was so vital to sustaining the Maya cities, it became woven into the heart of their story of creation:

> And here is the beginning of the conception of humans, and of the search for the ingredients of the human body. So they spoke, the Bearer, Begetter, the makers, and here their thoughts came out in clear light. They sought and discovered what was needed for human flesh . . .
>
> And these were the ingredients for the flesh of the human work, the human design, and the water was for the blood. It became human blood, and corn was also used by the Bearer, Begetter.

That's how the first humans were created by the great "mother-father," according to the **Popol Vuh**, the "Council Book" of the Maya. It's a sacred book like the Bible, the Torah, or the Koran. The Popol Vuh tells those who believe in the truth of its word that the ancient Maya people were made of the same stuff that makes up tortillas—the most important food of the ancient and present-day inhabitants of Yucatán. "We are the children of yellow-faced corn," goes a modern Maya saying. Did you ever hear the expression "You *are* what you *eat*?" If that's true, perhaps we could think of the Chinese as "people of rice," and the Inca as "potato people." How about us?

But before the creation, or the "sowing and the dawning," as the Maya called it, before the Bearer, Begetter could mold human flesh out of corn dough, the stage would have to be set. The world needed to be made safe. And so the gods sent the hero twins **Hunahpu** and **Xbalanque**, great blowgunner-hunters and ball players, to play a game of ball with the Lords of the **Xibalba**, the Underworld. Each of these hideous-looking deities is named after different things that harm us—like Stab Master, Pus Master, and Bloody Teeth. The twins defeated the Lords of the Xibalba and made the world a safer place to live in. Afterward, they rose into the sky to become the sun and the moon. Details of their underworld journey are also told on beautifully painted Maya pots.

We cannot overestimate the power of these traditional stories and the way they inspired a sense of belonging in the hearts of the Aztec and Maya people. Unfortunately, we don't know the creation story behind the great city of Cahokia. That's because the Indians who lived around the abandoned ruins knew nothing of who built it when asked by the first explorers. But the archaeological record offers some clues.

Maya artists painted vases with images of Hunahpu and Xbalanque, the hero twin gods who helped create the world.

Digging Cahokia was especially exciting. "In excavating near the base of the great temple mound of Cahokia," wrote one nineteenth-century archaeologist, "we found in a crumbling tomb of earth and stone a great number [more than one hundred] of burial vases . . . some of these were painted and there were also the paint-pots and dishes holding the colors." Since then, archaeologists have pulled dozens of objects out of the ground beneath the ancient city.

Big things come in small packages. The mid-1970s found a later generation of archaeologists busily excavating Mound 72, just outside the southern boundary of "Downtown Cahokia," which turns out to be one of the city's most important mounds. What lies inside tells us how the Cahokia people once practiced one of their most elaborate religious rituals to honor the dead.

Mound 72 is one of the more unusual of Cahokia's 120 large mounds. First, it's rectangular, measuring 140 x 70 feet. Second, it's the only mound that has a ridge on top. Third, it's twisted out of line from all the other mounds so that it points to the place where the sun sets on the first day of summer. Was it used as a sun-worshipping station, or perhaps to keep track of the season of the year? Maybe the Mississippian people deposited materials there that they used in their rituals? Archaeologist Melvin Fowler thought it would be a neat place to excavate.

After weeks of patient digging deeper and deeper into the past, one of Fowler's students' shovels made a crunching sound at the depth of one meter. It turned out to be the top of a huge pile of white arrowheads, an offering deliberately placed there. The archaeologists got out their spoons and dental picks for some close-up precision work. It would take weeks to carefully clear, remove, sort, and classify more than eight hundred arrowheads and the plaque with a carving of a winged man on it buried within them. Then, at a meter and a half, just under the arrowheads, the workers found a much larger object. It was a human bone, but so fragile a bone that when one of the students used his pick to remove the surrounding soil it crumbled to dust. The workers backed off. They tried to stabilize the bone, first with glue, then by pouring hot wax over fabric to cover it so it could hold its shape.

Analysis proved that they had unearthed the right thighbone of a forty-year-old man who had been showered in deposits of valuable objects. He was resting on a bed of twenty thousand shells in the shape of a falcon. In addition to the huge heaps of chert arrowheads placed around him were some chunkey stones. There were also other precious items, including sheets of mica carved in intricate shapes, and a three-foot-long roll of copper sheeting. The "Beaded Birdman," no doubt a member of Cahokia royalty, is just one of 280 people interred in Mound 72. It would take four years for Fowler and his team to carefully dig all of them up, and when they did the findings told of a violent episode. Among the occupants of Mound 72, Fowler discovered four headless men who also had no hands. Forensic anthropologists who later examined their bones found straight sharp cuts across the neck vertebrae at the base of the skull. They had been decapitated!

The "Beaded Birdman," a member of the Cahokia royalty, was buried on a bed of twenty thoussand shells in the shape of a falcon.

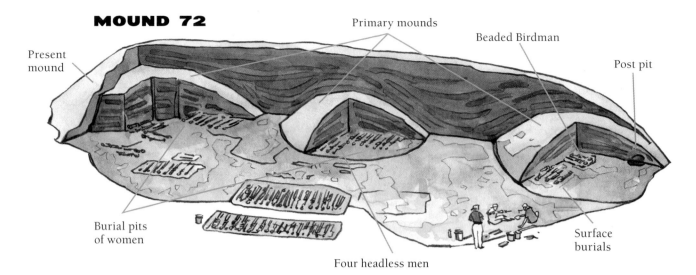

MOUND 72

Present mound

Primary mounds

Beaded Birdman

Post pit

Burial pits of women

Four headless men

Surface burials

In addition, archaeologists excavated four mass graves in Cahokia's Mound 72. They contained only young women, between fifteen and twenty-five years of age. In one of the graves, Fowler's students counted fifty women lined up in rows and stacked three deep. Dental experts determined that these women came from different gene pools. In other words, all of them could not have been citizens of Cahokia. Other graves in Mound 72 held high-status people. Prior to burial, they had been carefully wrapped in blankets and carried there on litters, or beds made out of thatch. Other people buried there seemed to be of lower status. To judge from the way they appeared, these victims must have been lined up at the edge of the pit, then struck from behind with a blunt instrument, such as a stone ax. Either they fell into the pit or they were pushed. Some of these victims were found with their fingers clawing at the sand up the side of the pit as if they were trying to climb out—they could not have been dead when they were buried. Some were reburials. People already dead for many years had been dug up and moved to Mound 72.

The layers of Mound 72 reveal that it is actually a buildup of more than a century of burials in three mounds that were joined together. The post pits marked the special places where the dead would be sent off to the afterworld. The small log building at the bottom was a *charnel house*, where they stored

59

the bodies. It was dismantled and the earliest reburials were placed in a mound on top of it. On top of that came the young women, the headless men, and, finally, the Beaded Birdman. The bodies found in Mound 72 are all that remain of sacrifices made by a specialized death cult. Like the Aztecs, the Cahokians had developed a highly organized religion that placed heavy emphasis on human sacrifice.

Studies of later Mississippian cultures help to illuminate how such a religion might have been practiced. The Natchez Indian rulers, descendants of the Cahokians, conducted sacrifices of some of their subjects. For example, at Fatherland site, more than a thousand miles down the Mississippi from Cahokia, and approximately five hundred years after the abandonment of Cahokia, a French explorer witnessed a gruesome ceremony in which sacrificial women were lined up. Each was given a plug of tobacco to chew to dull her senses. Then they were all strangled from behind and pushed into their graves. It may come as a surprise to us, but history records that some of these women willingly volunteered to accompany their leader into the afterworld as a way of demonstrating not only their high status in this world but also their strongly felt connection to their family ancestors in the next.

Precious goods—and people—from faraway places and times were put into Mound 72 to teach future Cahokia generations about their identity. To venerate ancestors like the Beaded Birdman, craftspeople offered the eight hundred arrowheads. People from distant villages dominated by Cahokia offered their young women, one of their most precious possessions, in tribute. All of these offerings formed part of a powerful great tradition. Mound 72 tells the story of the power relations of Cahokia and the role of religion in defining them. Because it contains the reburied bones of early ancestors alongside the body of their ruler, it records just how far back Cahokia authority goes.

Thanks to the electrical workers who discovered the Coyolxauhqui Stone

while laying cable in Mexico City, Mexican archaeologist Eduardo Matos Moctezuma organized a dig
in 1978 that would last fifteen years. He
and his team would unearth 135 offering
pits containing more than eight thousand
objects that Aztec worshippers had offered
in debt payments to their gods, Huitzilopochtli and Tlaloc, who were worshipped
in the two temples at the top of the Aztecs'
Great Temple, which the Aztecs called their
"human-made mountain." Among them were human
skulls pierced by flint knives, a skull made of crystal, a
giant statue of a bat god, delicately painted pottery, and
the celebrated "eagle warrior."

Matos and his students found tributes from the
forest—pumas, jaguars, birds; and from the ocean—
shells and fish. The objects originated in all the regions
of the Aztec empire, which at its peak in the fifteenth
century stretched from most of northern Mexico to the
coast of Guatemala. They discovered jades from the south and obsidian from
the north. There were artifacts from the past too: tiny stone Olmec heads that
were already more than a thousand years old when they were buried. The
archaeologists even found a number of beautiful ceramic pots the Aztecs
themselves had excavated at Teotihuácan. Just as modern American politi-
cians might say they stand on the principles of George Washington or Abra-
ham Lincoln, by extending their connection far back in time and far away
in distance, the Aztec rulers sought to establish their legitimacy. The offerings were debt payments. When a new emperor came to power, they would
reconstruct the temple, so that it now resembles a stack of pancakes, one
layer built on top of another. The archaeologists dug down through seven

A clay statue of an eagle warrior found during the excavation of the Great Temple in Tenochtítlan.

layers of offerings that had been deposited there each time the temple was rebuilt.

One of the Spanish chroniclers wrote this about the rituals King Moctezuma performed in the temple:

> On this day they flayed all the enemy prisoners, and dressed themselves in their skins; and they dedicated the festival to their god of sun and war. This festival fell when the sun was in the middle of [the temple of] Huitzilopochtli, which was the equinox, and because this was a little twisted, Moctezuma wished it torn down and straightened.

The first part of the statement, about warriors impersonating their gods by dressing up in the skins of their enemies, is fascinating enough, but the second part of the statement is even more telling.

Because the Aztec viewed their religious rites as dramas that people acted out, to make them work they needed to set the scene in the theater of ritual. The golden disk of the sun needed to be in the proper place at the correct time (evidently the first day of spring) when the people of Tenochtítlan gathered in the plaza at the foot of the temple to make their sacrifices to pay the debt to the sun god. And that was the job of the designers of the ceremonial architecture in these great cities—good timing makes for a great presentation. Conducting religious rituals in the proper manner was so important to the Aztecs that even the major buildings involved needed to be perfectly positioned.

Maya priests survey the position of Venus in preparation for building the Governor's Palace at Uxmal.

Like the Aztecs who claimed descent from antiquity, the Maya rulers claimed they were descended from ancestor gods who were believed to live in heaven. These gods controlled everything that took place in the sky. Seeking omens from the gods about the future of their crops, Maya court astronomers carefully charted the movement of the sun, moon, and planets and recorded them in their unique mathematical notations. Like their Aztec counterparts, Maya astronomers and keepers of the calendar were responsible for guaranteeing that the celestial gods would appear at the correct place and time to receive offerings in exchange for the omens they would deliver. Since people who lived in the tropics worshipped out of doors in the open plazas in front of the temples, honoring the sky gods in this kind of sacred space made sense to them.

One of the best examples of a celestially oriented temple in the Maya area is the House of the Governor at the ruins of Uxmal. Twisted out of line from the surrounding architecture, it was carefully erected so that its doorway aligned precisely with the most southerly rising point of the planet Venus. The Maya believed that Venus was the feathered serpent deity Kukulcán, the god of creativity. The frieze at the top of the temple (what you might call the "advertising space") is adorned with Venus symbols—the exact same ones found in a Maya codex used to predict the motion of Venus. Knowing when one of your gods will return from the underworld and then putting him on display would have made as big an impression on the citizens of Uxmal as the equinox sunrise over the Aztec temple. We can imagine Uxmal's people gathering in the predawn light to watch their king stand in the temple doorway to reunite with his ancestor god. Maya religion was so powerful that it had shaped the structure of their city.

If we dig deep enough, we may be surprised to discover that many of today's great American cities are not so different. Here is an interesting quote from a 1792 description of how our nation's capital, Washington, D.C., was laid out:

Mr. Ellicott drew a true meridional line, by celestial observation, which passes through the area intended for the Capitol. This line he crossed by another, running due east and west, which passes through the same area.

Eighteenth-century architects survey the land in preparation for building the U.S. Capitol in Washington, D.C., on a North/South-East/West axis.

It's part of the story about the heavenly arrangement of this special American city. The technique of drawing a line from the North Star, which marks the earth's axis, perpendicular to the sun's daily path, as mentioned in the quote, is reminiscent of Cahokia's plan.

Washington is America's most exquisitely planned city. The plan came out of an idea popular in late eighteenth-century France that envisioned what a great city ought to look like. It was conceived by the French-American architect Pierre Charles L'Enfant, a staff officer in General George Washington's Revolutionary army. The city named after America's first president was designed to rival the great cities of Europe. That's why it included rectangular axes and circles, where monuments of heroes and other great figures could be placed. Washington is laid out in the form of a perfect square ten miles on a side (the number of fingers on the hands of each of its inhabitants). The points of that square are precisely aligned to the directions north, south, east, and west. You could think of the U.S. Capitol as the pyramid that stands at the center, like ancient Teotihuácan's Pyramid of the Sun or Cahokia's Monk's Mound.

Whether monarchy or democracy, every government must establish its connection with the gods, wrote the French philosopher Jean Jacques Rousseau. And so, the city of Washington's spoked wheel, with its overlying grid pattern, which can be terribly confusing for pedestrians as well as for drivers, gives every tourist who visits it a sense of national identity. For example, Washington's processional way from the Capitol to the White House along Pennsylvania Avenue, and its inviting viewpoint from the Washington Monument along the Mall to the Capitol, is reminiscent of the ancient custom of laying out ceremonial ways and pilgrimage routes, such as Teotihuácan's Street of the Dead. Washington presents itself as a center of power. It is a junction point of sacred space and everyday space conceived in an enlightened age. As Uxmal was to the Maya, Washington is every American's heavenly city.

The huacas in Cuzco's ceque system were especially important in the way they bonded people together socially through religious practices. A huaca could be a carved rock, a bend in a stream, an ancient tree, or a *puquio* (a natural spring). Just as the Aztecs made offerings to pay back their gods, it was the duty of all the people of Tahuantinsuyu (Cuzco) to feed the earth goddess Pachamama. Different people in the community made offerings at the appropriate huacas at specified times, so that mother earth would provide them with the water they needed to grow their crops. Here's a Spanish chronicler's detailed description of just one of Cuzco's 328 huacas:

> The seventh *huaca* (counting outward from the Coricancha) of the eighth *ceque* of **Chinchaysuyu** (the northwest suyu) was called ***sucanca***. It was a hill by way of which the water channel from **Chinchero** comes. On it, there were two towers as an indication that when the sun arrives there, they had to begin to plant. The sacrifice which was made there was directed to the sun, asking him to arrive there on that hill at the time which would be appropriate to planting and they sacrificed to him sheep, clothing, and miniature lambs of gold and silver.

This passage tells us a lot about Inca religion. First, the chronicler is probably confusing lambs with llamas. The people of the Andes domesticated llamas. They used them to carry heavy loads up and down the steep hills. Llamas were vital to Andean culture not only as pack animals but also as a source of food. Llama herders decorated the ears of their animals and they held special ceremonies to make llama sacrifices. Remember: You sacrifice what is *most* valuable to you! When llamas were sacrificed, a *diviner* would cut open the animal, pull out the internal organs—and "read" them. The Inca diviner was especially interested in the lungs. That's odd, because we think of the brain as our major source of contact with the outside world. Europeans once thought of the heart in this way. Andean diviners would look at the veins, indentations, and changes in color of the lung tissue to read the omens from the gods.

Second, the quote has to do with agriculture. It tells us that water was important. In a vertical environment like the high Andes, that's not surprising. Controlling water would have been of paramount importance. The huaca named sucanca, along with other huacas, is a part of an "environmental clock." Inca rulers erected a number of sun pillar–huacas that marked the exact times of year to plant in the different altitudes around Cuzco. Third, the quote tells us about social relationships. It implies thatspecific things needed to be sacrificed at specific places. Each huaca wasassigned worship by different classes of individuals in Inca society, ranging from royalty, people of mixed blood, commoners, even visitors to the city. Everyone participated.

Mummification also played an important role in Andean religions. One of the most amazing mummy finds was made in 1995. Explorer/anthropologist Johan Reinhard and his guide Miguel Zarate weren't looking for mummies at all when they climbed toward the 21,000-foot summit of Mount **Ampato** in the southern Andes. The two were trying to get a good

Facing page: Pillars on a hillside overlooking Cuzco lined up with the sunset when it was time to plant crops. Andean farmers made sacrifices here to reciprocate for a fertile crop. Above: A miniature silver llama used as a sacrifice to the gods.

view of a neighboring volcanic peak. What they found was even more spectacular than an erupting volcano. Sitting exposed on the ice was the mummified body of a twelve- to fourteen-year-old girl. Melting and shifting ice had uncovered her original burial site, but the mummy had survived. Thanks to having been frozen solid for more than five hundred years, her body was in a perfect state of preservation. Her skin, though dried out, still showed veins, even tiny hairs—and she still had her eyelashes. She looked as if she was sleeping. The explorers named the mummy Juanita. Analysis of Juanita's body showed that she was hit on the head with a heavy object before being placed there—she was probably a victim of child sacrifice.

The Inca believed that the mountains were their ancestors who had been turned to stone. Mountain spirits were very powerful. They were responsible for snowstorms and landslides. And they gave the Inca water for their crops. For all of these reasons, the Inca believed the mountains deserved the most precious of sacrifices, like the Ice Maiden.

Like the people of Cahokia, the Inca of Peru seem to have had a particular fascination with the dead. Because preserving their ancestors was important to them, making mummies is part of an Andean heritage that goes back more than five thousand years. The Chinchoro people, who lived on the coast of Peru more than six thousand years before the Inca, may have been the first people in the world to fabricate mummies. They did it first by dismembering their dead. They took out all the organs; then they packed the body cavity with fiber and clay and put in wood supports to keep the spine straight. Before stitching the body back together, they

Juanita

68

added a layer of clay to the skull. Then they painted and decorated the mummy and put a wig on it. This made the dead more presentable to their visiting relatives when they were brought out on social occasions, a practice that was very popular in the city of Cuzco.

We may find the descriptions of ancient religious rituals gruesome. We might conclude that the Inca, the Aztecs, and the people of Cahokia were simply bloodthirsty, brutal savages. But before we judge them, we need to understand what sacrifice meant *to them*. It's all about giving up something that really matters as a way of reinforcing what you truly believe in. For example, we know that the Aztecs believed the gods once sacrificed in order to create the sun to light our world. So there's a relationship between the act of human sacrifice and the story of creation. The world needs to be renewed over and over again and only *people* have the power to make this happen. So, the sacrificial ceremonies at the Great Temple link the people directly to the process of renewal, not just of the world, but of life itself. Like the Cahokians, the Aztecs offered special things, such as flowers, tobacco smoke, the first fruits of the harvest, and fresh blood, in exchange for abundant rain, good crops, and sound health. They were a reverent people and human sacrifice was the highest religious act they could perform. Like the Inca of Cuzco, they called themselves the children of the sun, because their task, their "burden" as they would say, was to keep the sun on its course and their delicate world in balance and harmony. Regardless of what religion you might practice, reading this chapter should have convinced you that being religious in America's first great cities was nothing like our going to church, temple, or mosque. But if you think about it, all religions, including the exotic ones we've encountered, challenge people to think beyond personal affairs and daily life. They also teach us to offer what is precious to us, whether it is our time or our material goods, in order to strengthen our beliefs. Religion also teaches believers to respect the powers and forces in the universe that are greater than themselves. Perhaps today's Americans are not so different from their ancient counterparts.

Following two pages: Aztec priests sacrifice a prisoner at the Great Temple.

5

LESSONS FROM THE CRUMBLED RUINS

All of the ancient American cities had large, concentrated populations.
They all had specialized labor and large-scale production of crafts. Urban so-
cieties were class structured and all of them created political, military, and
religious functionaries. They developed systems of taxation and tribute to
control the distribution of goods. Rulers built monumental works, temples,
and palaces, which helped foster a shared identity. Cities developed mathematics, calendars, and in some cases, a form of writing to create their histories, to keep track of material goods, and to establish when and under what
conditions to conduct religious rituals. Given this impressive recipe for success, why have all these great ancient cities vanished from the American landscape? What happened that caused them to fail? This is perhaps the greatest
lesson that we can learn from people of the past.

The larger a city becomes and the more people of diverse ethnic groups
and locations that it attempts to control, the more likely it is that the system

Facing page: The Spanish conquistador Francisco Pizarro promised to spare King Atahualpa's life if a
Coricancha chamber was piled seven-feet high with treasure.

will break down and decline. For example, the Aztecs' own misdeeds led to their undoing. King Ahuitzotl had stretched Tenochtítlan's domination to the breaking point. Offering nothing in return to those he subjugated, his violence and lust for sacrificial blood to replenish the gods made him a lot of enemies, like the Tlaxcálans, who lived near the coastal area where Cortés landed. When Cortés arrived in 1519, with an invading army of five hundred men accompanied by cannon and horses in search of New World treasures, the Spaniards took advantage of the situation by allying themselves with the disgruntled Tlaxcálans and the rulers of other native towns that had been brutally suppressed by the Aztec empire. By the time the allies arrived in the capital city after a long uphill march from the coast, they numbered fifty thousand. On top of that, Spanish cannon and horses were vastly superior to the bows and arrows wielded by the Aztecs. The Spaniards faced a much weaker ruler in King Moctezuma II, a successor to Ahuitzotl. Moctezuma would later tell his conquerors that he had seen a bad omen in the sky, most likely a comet. It bled fire and looked like a giant wound, he said. The king seemed unsure of how to deal with these strange-looking, bearded white people. At first he welcomed them as returning gods, but when he realized their evil intentions, he expelled them. The Spaniards responded by laying siege to the city. After two years and thousands of lives lost in skirmishes, the Aztecs, their spirits broken, gave up their city, and great Tenochtítlan was quickly plundered into ruin.

Those who didn't die by sword or rifle perished from smallpox and other diseases to which the natives were not immune, brought across the Atlantic by the intruders. But unlike North America, where few colonists mixed blood with the Indians, the Aztec legacy lives on in the descendants of the natives, who intermarried with the Spaniards. Today four out of five Mexican people share the blood of two continents.

A similar misfortune fell on ancient Cuzco-Tahuantinsuyu. Once again the Spaniards came at the right time and they took advantage of political developments. The Inca empire was divided by sibling rivalry. King Atahualpa ruled the southern empire based in Cuzco while his brother Huascar led the capital of the northern faction in Quito. The two kingdoms were on the verge of a brotherly civil war when Francisco Pizarro docked on the Pacific coast of Peru in 1532.

Cortés's army of conquistadors allied with local enemies of the Aztec to lay siege to the city of Tenochtítlan.

Six million Inca descendants spread throughout Peru and Bolivia still speak Quechua, the language of the Inca. Of the city itself, few structures survived the Spanish. Only the lower rooms of the Coricancha survive. That's because the Spaniards dismantled much of the structure and used its exquisitely carved granite block foundation as the base for their buildings. They built the Roman Catholic Church of Santo Domingo directly on top of the Inca ruins. That helped convert the Inca to the Spaniards' Christian religion, because it venerated the same place that was sacred to the Inca. In the five centuries since then, earthquakes have toppled the church a few times, but the sturdy lower walls of the Coricancha remain solidly earthquake-proof. Stone blocks made by Inca craftsmen were so perfectly carved that they needed no mortar to hold them together.

While the conquest of the Aztec and Inca empires, so sudden, tragic, and shocking, happened because of the intrusion of outsiders at opportune times, the much earlier demise of Cahokia and the Maya cities resulted from other causes that played out over a longer time period. Cahokia is now long gone. Only faint traces of their lineage remain in the blood of American Indians; but there is a history lesson in the archaeological excavation of Mound 72: no civilization's power lasts forever.

The lower layers of the Cahokia excavations, which must come from an earlier period of history, generally contain caches from a broad area of great wealth. Higher layers, made up of more recent tribute offerings, show successively smaller caches with fewer items in each. This is a sign that, as time went on, luxuries became less abundant, which implies that Cahokia influence had dwindled. But why? By the thirteenth century, Cahokia was no longer a wealthy and prosperous city. It had fallen into decay long before the Europeans got there. Climatologists have determined that the early thirteenth century was a time of drought in much of what we now call the United States. The scarcity of natural resources may have triggered unrest and maybe even war among the competing Mississippian towns.

Their bones tell us that these later people also developed health problems from an unbalanced diet that was becoming too heavily based on corn. All of these factors led to a gradual breakup of the city. As the population decreased, those who left probably blended in with smaller towns located on higher land more distant from the bottomlands of the river. By the fourteenth century, less than a dozen generations before the first white explorers arrived, Mound 72, Monk's Mound, and all the other mounds that once made up ancient North America's greatest city, were already overgrown—so overgrown that Lewis and Clark, and Marquette and Joliet, never would have had a chance of finding the lost city, even if they had sailed the mighty Mississippi a hundred years earlier.

Likewise, by the time the Spanish conquistadors came to Mesoamerica,

Facing page: The stone blocks of Coricancha's lower walls still stand today, and serve as a foundation for the Church of Santo Domingo in Cuzco.

the Maya pyramids were long abandoned. They had been swallowed up by the jungle. After thriving for more than five hundred years under dynasties ruled by powerful kings and queens, the great Maya cities began to decline in the eighth century. The inscriptions, together with other evidence from archaeology, tell the sad story of the collapse of the Maya civilization. For example, we know that at Copán, Yax Pasah, unlike his predecessors, had big problems. He was starting to lose his grip on the throne. If you compare his relatively plain-looking stela with that of his grandfather, you can begin to see a decline in Maya works of art. Diminished specialization is usually an early sign of a civilization in decay.

The stela of Maya ruler Waxak-Lahun-Ubah-Kawil (left) is much more impressive than that of his grandson, Yax Pasah.

Bones uprooted from Maya burials dated to the time of Yax Pasah's rule tell us that many people were undernourished. Evidently Copán was having a hard time feeding its fast-growing population of 25,000, because of a widespread drought. Nutrients were disappearing from the soil from over-farming. Inscriptions on some of the king's monuments in the area around Copán suggest that he may have been forced into sharing power with local rulers. Maybe his vassals were telling him: We are tired of paying you tribute with our offerings of food when we barely have enough to feed our own families. And we can't afford to offer you our labor to build huge stone houses adorned with sculpture for all your close relatives while we go hungry.

The archaeological record tells what happened next. The last building in central Copán's great acropolis carries a date of AD 800. Excavating trash pits in its rooms dating from that period, archaeologists have concluded that the people abandoned the big downtown buildings. They transferred the royal residence to a much smaller structure on the outskirts of Copán, which carries much later dates in its inscriptions. But that structure was burned in the middle of the ninth century, possibly by peasants who revolted against the king. After Yax Pasah, there are no more Copán inscriptions. He was the last ruler of his dynasty. The once powerful king would eventually meet a sad fate. He was decapitated by Cauac Sky, ruler of the neighboring city of Quirigua. What about his people? Most fanned out from the valley in search of better land to farm.

Should we blame the fall of Copán on unfortunate King Yax Pasah? For centuries, the Maya had planted their corn, beans, squash, and chili on small plots of land. Before the next rainy season, they cut down and burned the dried out remains. That would kill off any insects and give the crops good fertilizer for the next growing season. But this "slash and burn" agriculture also killed off many of the soil's nutrients. When a field no longer produced, farmers would cultivate adjacent areas farther from the city center. By the time of the Copán crisis, some farmers needed to spend an entire day walking just to get to their crops. The pollen record from soil cores tells us that by AD 1000 Copán farmers had cut down every tree in the valley. They had exhausted the soil far up the hillsides. So you can't blame one king, much less a hurricane or a mega-drought for Copán's downfall. What happened at Copán also happened at Palenque, Tikal, and Calakmul. With an assist from nature, the Maya did it to themselves.

But Maya greatness would not perish—at least not yet. Instead, their great tradition spread northward. New cities like Chichén Itzá, Uxmal, and Mayapán flourished for more than three hundred years after the great collapse in the southern lowlands. Many people still came back to the courtyards and abandoned palaces of fallen cities like Copán, Tikal, Calakmul, and Palenque. They came in pilgrimages to worship because their grandparents had told them of the impressive palaces that were built there to honor their ancestral gods. The people knew these palaces were still sacred, even if they had forgotten how to read the dates and inscriptions on the stelae.

What finally happened to the Maya who abandoned their cities? Most of them established smaller, less centralized communities. Today, there are more than two million Maya people spread out over Guatemala, Honduras, El Salvador, Belize, and parts of southern Mexico. They speak twenty-nine different dialects of the language of their ancestors. And the Maya ruins have been restored by archaeologists so that we can visit them today. They serve as remembrances of the grandeur of a glorious past. Though the great Maya cities are abandoned, remains of their great tradition, like the traditions of many of America's other great cities, still live on.

The slash and burn methods of Maya farmers depleted natural resources and quickly exhausted the soil.

History's lessons are many. While the great Aztec and Inca cities had the misfortune to become victims of the Spanish conquest of the Americas, the Maya and the people of Cahokia offer excellent examples of the need to manage resources. Both cities outstripped the ability of the surrounding environment to support their ever-increasing populations. The increasing demand on the dwindling food supply, aided by the misfortune of a prolonged drought, took its toll. What made matters worse, especially for Cahokia, was their strong dependence on a single crop: corn. Neither civilization seems to have developed a plan for the future when it came to subsistence.

Size, sound leadership, specialized guilds, impressive architecture and sculpture, organized religion and its attending ritual—all of these traits that make for a successful city—don't matter very much if the basic needs of life are not being met. Public dissatisfaction leads to revolt, and cities decline. City life disappears as people leave in search of places where their needs might be better met. And so as old cities fall into ruin, new ones grow up. Knowing why cities fail may be as important as understanding how they succeed.

When future historians examine our culture, what will they think? When archaeologists of the future dig up the remains of our cities, what will they find? Ruined stone buildings, steel bridges, and bronze monuments—maybe even a few statues honoring famous people. They will probably find lots of plastic bottles and tin cans, too. What else will they find? And what will they make of us?

Following pages: The remains of Inca stonework at Sacsayhuaman on the hillside overlooking modern Cuzco.

PRONUNCIATIONS

Ahuitzotl (ah weet-tul)

alpaca (al-pack'-uh)

Ampato (ahm-páh-toe)

Atahualpa (ah-tuh-wahl'-puh)

Atzcapotzalco (ats-kah-poat-sahl'-coh)

Axayacatl (ah-shah-yah'-cot-tul)

Calakmul (kah-lock-moól)

calmecac (kahl-meh-cahk')

ceques (seh'-kas)

Cerén (suh-rain')

Chichén Itzá (chee-chain'-eet-sah')

Chinchaysuyu (cheen-chahy-sóo-yoo)

Chinchero (cheen-chay'-roh)

Cholula (cho-loo'-lah)

codices (cóe-duh-sees)

Copán (coe-pahn')

Coricancha (kor-ee-kahn'–chuh)

cuicacalli (kwee-kah-kah'-lee)

Cuzco (coós-coh)

huacas (wah'-kuhs)

Hunahpu (hoon-ah-pooh')

Ixtaccihuati (eesh-tah-see'-wat-tul)

Izcalli (eesh-cah'-lee)

llama (yah'-muh)

manos (mah'-noes)

Mayapán (my-uh-pahn')

metates (muh-tah'-tays)

Moctezuma (mock-tuh-sóo-muh)

moieties (moy'-uh-tees)

Mount Ampato (ahm-pah'-toh)

Nahuatl (náh-wat-tul)

Pachamama (pah-chah-máh-muh)

Palenque (puh-len'-kay)

Petén (pay-ten')

Piedras Negras (pe-ay'-drus-náy-grus)

Popocatépetl (poe-poe-cuh-tay'-pet-uhl)

Popol Vuh (poe-pull-voóh)

Proskouriakoff (pro-skoo'-re-uh-koff)

puna (poo'-nah)

puquio (poo'-kee-oh)

Quetzal (ket'-sahl)

quipu (keé-poo)

quipucamayoc (kée–poo-kuh-mahy'-ock)

Runa Simi (rooh'-nuh-see'-mee)

sucanca (soo-kahn'-kuh)

Tahuantinsuyu (tah-wahn-teen-soo'-yoo)

teosinte (tay-oh-sin'-tay)

Teotihuácan (tay-oh-tee-wah'-kahn)

teponaztli (tay-peo-náhs-tlee)

Texcoco (tets-koh'-koh)

Tezcatlipoca (Tets-kaht-lee-poh'-kuh)

tianquiztli (tee-ahn-kees'-tlee)

Tikal (tee-káhl)

Uaxactún (wah-shank-toon')

Uxmal (oosh-máhl)

Waxak-Lahun-Ubah-Kawil (wah-shókk-la-
hóon-ooh-báh-kah-wéel)

Xbalanque (shbah-lahn-kay')

Xibalba (she-bahl-báh)

Yax K'uk' Mo' (yosh-kook-moh')

Yax Pasah (yósh-puh-sáh)

Yollopíltic (yoh-loh-peel'-teek)

SOURCE NOTES

Every writer owes those of his profession who paved the roadway. My multidiscipline is fortunate to house a number of professionals—archaeologists, historians, art historians, anthropologists, and folklorists—who have written works that appeal to an audience outside the scholarly journals. Among the works I have drawn on in producing *Buried Beneath Us* are the many editions of Michael D. Coe's *The Maya* (London: Thames & Hudson, 1966–2011). The Smithsonian Series "Exploring the Ancient World" (1992–1996), to which I contributed the volume *Ancient Astronomers* (1993), provided five volumes: Elizabeth Hill Boone's *The Aztec World*, T. Patrick Culbert's *Maya Civilization*, James Meltzer's *Search for the First Americans*, Linda S. Cordell's *Ancient Pueblo Peoples*, and Anthony P. Andrews's *First Cities*. My colleagues in Native American Studies at *National Geographic* magazine produced two very informative full-length books: Gene S. Stuart's *America's Ancient Cities* (1989) and *Mysteries of the Maya: The Rise, Glory, and Collapse of an Ancient Civilization* (August, 2008). I also drew from Johanna Broda, David Carrasco, and Edwardo Matos Moctezuma's *The Great Temple of Tenochtitlan: Center and Periphery in the Aztec World* (Berkeley: University of California Press, 1987), David Carrasco and Scott Sessions's *Daily Life of the Aztecs* (Westport: Greenwood, 2008), Michael E. Moseley's *The Incas and Their Ancestors: The Archaeology of Peru* (London: Thames & Hudson, 1992), John Hyslop's *Inca Settlement Planning* (Austin: University of Texas Press, 1990), and Brian S. Bauer's *The Sacred Landscape of the Inca: The Cusco Ceque System* (Austin: University of Texas Press, 1998).

Reading Jeffrey F. Meyer's *Myths in Stone: Religious Dimensions of Washington, DC* (Berkeley: University of California Press, 2001) inspired me to compare the Native American cities with our own Washington, D.C., and Biloine Whiting Young and Melvin L. Fowler's book on the Cahokia excavations, *Cahokia, the Great Native American Metropolis* (Urbana: University of Illinois Press, 1999), helped give me a sense of the work-a-day nature of the archaeological profession. I also found some of the older general survey texts helpful because they gave me a feel for the way the discovery process changes with time and technological advancements. Among these are *Mysteries of the Ancient Americas* (Readers Digest, 1986), *Atlas of Ancient America* (Equinox, 1986), and *America's Fascinating Indian Heritage* (Readers Digest, 1978).

Finally, I have consulted numerous articles on archaeology in the ancient Americas in issues of *Archaeology* magazine dating back to 1973; the same for select issues of *National Geographic* magazine.

ACKNOWLEDGMENTS

I habitually extend my gratitude to Diane Janney, my assistant for more than a decade on a dozen book projects, and Lorraine Aveni, my "firewall" editor on everything I have written. I am also indebted to Colgate student Samantha Newmark, who carefully critiqued earlier drafts of this work. Among my other students who have shown a special interest in children's literature, I count Tina Buzak, now a dedicated middle school teacher. Finally, I extend my thanks to my colleague and collaborator David Carrasco, for his insight and wisdom on other collaborative works for children, to Leonardo Lopez Luján, my informant on all things Aztec, and to my good friend and agent for more than twenty-five years, Faith Hamlin.

INDEX

Numbers in **bold** indicate pages with illustrations